MW01680922

TRANSFORM YOUR **LEADERSHIP**

ABOUT THE AUTHOR

My name is Marguerite Orane.

"Were you just born happy?" I am often asked. With a chuckle, I respond: "Maybe, but I do have to work very hard at it."

I believe everyone in the world has an inner capacity for joy. Dedicated to changing the way we live and work, I coach and facilitate CEOs and their leadership teams in realising the value that joy and happiness at work bring to people and profits. My experience as a CEO from age 23, an entrepreneur, a Harvard MBA, a deep commitment to my inner journey, and my curiosity about the mysteries and delights of the world are the foundation of this work.

I am proud, loud, and unapologetically Jamaican. I currently live in Toronto, Canada, with my joy sidekick Sushi, but travel extensively to joyfully explore and delight in our amazing world.

For more about me, visit: **www.margueriteorane.com**

Transform Your Leadership:

8 Essential Practices for Leading With

JOY

MARGUERITE ORANE

First published in Canada 2026 by
Free and Laughing Inc.
509 Beecroft Road,
Toronto, ON M2N0A3,
Canada

www.margueriteorane.com
Email: *marguerite@margueriteorane.com*

ISBN: 978-1-9994078-2-7 (Print)
ISBN: 978-1-9994078-3-4 (eBook)

Cover and book design by Robert Harris (*robertcharris62@gmail.com*)
Cover graphics by Chris Cushman (*cjcushman@gmail.com*)
Edited by Cecile Clayton (*cecile.clayton@gmail.com*)

Set in Scala 11.3/16

FOR LEADERS WHO SEEK

Also by **Marguerite Orane:**

Free and Laughing: Spiritual Insights in Everyday Moments, (2008)

Forget it! What's the Point? Letting Go and Claiming Joy (2018)

CONTENTS

JOY is much bigger than happiness. While happiness is often seen as being dependent on external circumstances, **JOY** is not.

—ARCHBISHOP DESMOND TUTU

INTRODUCTION

The genesis of this book is a video of my dog Sushi. I had posted a video of her on Instagram, spinning around in complete abandon and joy upon my return home (from taking out the garbage). She was whirling so dervishly that I couldn't keep her in the video frame. The fact that I was laughing so hard didn't help either. As imperfect as it was from a videographer's point of view, the video was perfect in depicting the joy that was clearly evident in both of us.

Fellow author, Roland Watson-Grant, made a comment on the post that shook my world:

JOY NEEDS SPACE

His comment triggered reflection on the coaching work I do with my Executive Leadership clients and their teams, and how much of it is simply helping them to clear space. I didn't realise it then, but what I have been doing is helping them clear space for joy. And that's the first premise of this book: that for us to be joyful, we must create space. There can be little or no joy where there is clutter. This applies as much to our closets as to the way we spend our time at work in back-to-back meetings, a deluge of emails, and crises by the minute. Joy needs space, and nowhere is this more pressing than at work.

But why in the world do we want and even need joy at work? This leads to my second premise:

JOY IS A SERIOUS VALUE PROPOSITION

When I first started on my journey of deliberate practice of Joy at Work, there was very little research on the value of joy. How would I convince CEOs that joy was of great value to their bottom line? How could I convince them that joy wasn't just some touchy-feely, warm and fuzzy "HR thing" that only distracted from "serious work"?

Fortunately, there is research that supports my belief and provides strong evidence. My introduction to formal research was the January/February 2012 issue of the Harvard Business Review, its cover emblazoned with a yellow smiley face, and the Title: "The Value of Happiness". I still have the copy I purchased in the Miami airport, now faded and dog-eared, as it has travelled the world with me while I meet and share the value of joy with clients and audiences, and all who will give me an ear. Shawn Anchor, in his article "Positive Intelligence" in that HBR issue, cited three research findings that stood out for me, which I often quote and that, to my knowledge, have not been debunked in the ensuing years:

In a sweeping meta-analysis of 225 academic studies, Sonja Lyubomirsky, Laura King, and Ed Diener found that happy employees have, on average, 31% higher productivity; their sales are 37% higher; and their creativity is three times higher.

My follow-up question to CEOs when I share the findings is: Which of your current initiatives is giving you this return on investment?

In recent years, the study of employee engagement, happiness, engagement, and joy, and their impact on business outcomes is burgeoning, validating many of the findings stated in the HBR issue. For example, in 2023, Forbes magazine reported on a study published in Management Science that found a direct, positive link between happiness and productivity – strikingly, each one-unit increase in happiness (on a scale of 0–10) led to a 12% increase in productivity.

And my third premise?

JOY IS A CHOICE

What is joy, and why would you choose it, especially in a world with so much suffering and unhappiness? The answer is personal and unique to each of us. Robert Holden, in his book "Be Happy" writes: "Joy is impossible to define, but it can be described".

I, too, have struggled to define joy. I have questions that I haven't yet been able to answer:

- By defining joy, do we limit it?
- Is it something that we will know only when we feel it?
- Is joy being or doing?
- Can we really choose joy in all circumstances?

Here's where I am with what joy means to me:

Choosing joy means that I am deciding to live from a place of being positive and grounded. It means being the eye of calm in the storm. Being joyful and leading joyfully allows me to see opportunities in crises, to be of help to others – like clients, co-workers, and the community – to feel calm and peaceful, no matter what.

This book invites you to explore your own definition of joy, not from a theoretical place, but from deep introspection, practice, and adjustment. Until it just FEELS right and you know that it can be nothing but joy.

ABOUT THE 8 PRACTICES

This is a practical book. There are 8 Essential Practices, with exercises for Daily Joy at the conclusion of each chapter.

These practices have been developed from nearly 50 years' experience as a leader – running organisations, serving on boards, teaching and coaching in leadership. And also, from observing leaders in action. My adventures, particularly summitting Mt. Kilimanjaro, trekking the Himalayas, and visiting Machu Picchu, have provided deep insights into the universality of joy and great leadership across cultures. I have experienced the utmost joy of coaching leaders and observing their transformation as they embrace the practices, do the work, and manifest the results. It is mind-blowing, spine-tingling, goose-bumpy and eye-watering for me to witness. It is the work I am meant to do, and it's my absolute delight to share with you these 8 Essential Practices for Leading with Joy in this book.

The Eight Practices:

- The Practice of Reflection
- The Practice of Grounding Your Day in Joy
- The Practice of Silence

- The Practice of Making Peace With Time
- The Practice of Forgiveness
- The Practice of Acceptance
- The Practice of Asking for Help
- The Practice of Celebration

Are these the only practices that can help you lead with joy? Not at all. Consider them a launchpad for your learning and adventure into the uncharted territory of your own journey of leading with joy.

The book is designed for you to tackle one practice at a time, slowly and patiently, as you transform your leadership. Whilst you can start with any of the practices, I highly recommend that you do Joy Practice #1 first. You can also use the book as a reference. Whenever you have a problem, i.e., something impeding your joy, find a chapter that offers a solution and work on that until the problem is diminished, or even solved.

WHAT YOU NEED FOR YOUR JOURNEY OF LEADING WITH JOY

- A mind open to transforming your beliefs about leadership and how you behave as a leader;
- A spirit of inquiry to observe, reflect on, and question everything you thought you knew to be true;

- Daily commitment – this is not a one-off, quick-hit hack. Truly being joyful and leading joyfully requires committing to daily practice;
- A journal to record your reflections and experiences, to be the channel through which your subconscious becomes conscious, and to be your closest and trusted confidante;
- A willingness to be courageous and vulnerable, to step out of your own and society's *status quo*, to put your heart on the line, to be open to making and learning from mistakes, and to engage in a journey that is yours to create, own, and revel in – a journey that is uniquely YOU.

Now, let's get started on your journey of leading with joy.

. . . REMEMBER:

Joy needs space

Joy is a serious value proposition

Joy is a choice

1 The Practice of Reflection

2 The Practice of Grounding Your Day in Joy

3 The Practice of Silence

4 The Practice of Making Peace With Time

5 The Practice of Forgiveness

6 The Practice of Acceptance

7 The Practice of Asking for Help

8 The Practice of Celebration

ESSENTIAL PRACTICE #1:

REFLECTION

"The
unexamined
life is not
worth living."

—ATTRIBUTED TO THE PHILOSOPHER SOCRATES

1

I was 23 years old, with a cherubic face that made me look more like 16, all of 5 feet tall, when I assumed the mantle of Managing Director of my family's door manufacturing business. I struggled with how best to lead the group of 70 hardened, rambunctious male employees, aware that I needed to be seen as strong, assertive, and no walk-over. But fresh out of university, I had neither guide nor template and certainly, no experience.

Desperate to assert myself and aware of the urgency of taking control, I sought examples of successful leadership that I thought I could emulate. I had heard about one of the most respected business leaders in Jamaica who would, every now and then, rant and rave with a few choice curse words. So, one day I tried it – I dropped the "F" word in a loud, aggressive tone, eyes blazing, back rigid and erect as if I were Napoleon himself. I can still see the mouths of the men drop to the floor in shock. It had the intended effect. On them.

But not on me. It was a self-inflicted slap in the face. It felt wrong. Upon reflection days, weeks, and even months later, I realised that it wasn't me, not my style, nor the type of leader I wanted to be. Pity I had not thought it through before, as I am certain I would have made a different choice.

"Soft skills" have emerged as a very valid, empowering, and effective way of leading that gets, and even exceeds, expected results. The term originated in the USA in the 1960s, surprisingly from that most traditionally masculine of places – the military. The top brass began to realise that the key skills for effectively mobilising soldiers lay less in technical skills, as important as they are, and more in the skills of collaboration and interpersonal relationship building.

Over time, the term has become popular in the corporate world. Better yet, the practice has become more prevalent with the emergence of Emotional Intelligence (EI) as conceptualised by Daniel Goleman. Goleman identifies four competences of Emotional Intelligence:

- self-awareness
- self-management
- social awareness or empathy
- social skills (which very closely align with soft skills)

My own observation and experience over many years of interacting with and coaching leaders at all levels have led me to conclude that the higher one climbs the ladder, the greater the importance of Emotional Intelligence (EI). One can delegate technical skills, but not the soft skills.

It is no accident that Self-Awareness is the first precept of EI – it is the foundation. Without it, one cannot practice the other aspects. Many of us, particularly in the busyness of our work, are on autopilot, carrying out actions with little awareness. There is no space between a situation and our reaction to it. No space to observe, be aware of ourselves, and choose our response.

The space between a situation and our response is space for joy.

The question is: How do we improve our self-awareness?

It is difficult to observe ourselves in the moment. "Being present" is tough, requiring us to be aware of our thoughts, words, and actions as they are happening. Most of the time, our minds are focussed on a multitude of memories (the past) and imagining the future. Becoming more self-aware requires the conscious, deliberate practice of self-reflection. Reflecting on our actions is a portal to learning and transformation of our leadership. What did we do; why did we do it? What was the impact? What could we have done differently? These are simple, yet important and profound questions to reflect on every day. Over time, regular reflection will close the gap between our actions and awareness, allowing us to self-correct

The space
between a
situation and
our response is
space for joy.

in the moment, and even to choose proactively. We move from unconscious reaction to conscious action.

To make self-reflection a deliberate practice for joyful leadership, I advocate daily journalling.

Journalling at its most basic, is the act of writing down your thoughts, feelings, and insights. It's a very private act – just you and the paper. It is a space of freedom to express yourself uninhibited by the eyes, opinions, and judgement of others. Your journal is your best friend that doesn't talk back, except in your own inner wisdom.

Journalling has many benefits. It reduces stress and anxiety. Things happen. But stress happens when we keep replaying the thing that happened in our minds. And we also get anxious when we live in the future by anticipating what could happen. Journalling allows us to clear our thoughts, to create distance between what happened and our reaction to it, and between what we think could happen in the future. It also organises the mind. The act of writing things down tends to bring order to jumbled thoughts, and this brings clarity. By unleashing our innermost thoughts in our journal before sharing them with someone, we avoid saying the wrong thing or saying it in a way that may hurt. And this leads to healthier relationships.

Journalling gives you the freedom to express yourself with no limits. It can be as simple as grabbing a piece of paper, a pen, or a pencil and starting to write. I advocate handwriting rather than digital journalling. Observe for yourself the difference when you write by hand – the swoop and swirl of

To make
self-reflection
a deliberate
practice for
joyful leadership,
I advocate
**daily
journalling**.

your hand holding the pen to the paper, slowing down and allowing your thoughts to flow, versus the staccato of your fingers on the keyboard. Neurologically, there's a difference – handwriting engages your fine motor skills to manage the pen, trace each letter, and discern how much pressure to apply and the direction in which to write. Contrast that to typing, in which your fingers don't know the difference between the letter "a" and "z". If you haven't written by hand in a while, try it and notice what happens. Even my tech-savvy coaching clients report a distinct difference in their handwritten journalling practice.

Interestingly, despite all these benefits, and despite my begging, pleading, compelling, and my passionate, glowing commendations, journalling is the practice my clients resist the most. The fundamental challenge is fear, expressed as concern that someone might find their journal and read what they wrote. For some, it might go deeper – it's a fear of facing and coming to terms with their subconscious, deeply held and buried beliefs, memories, and mistakes. This is uncomfortable, disorienting, and disruptive to one's neatly curated *status quo.* But it's that same *status quo* that keeps them stuck and unable to move forward as they wish. Frank and honest self-reflection requires courage to move from a place of seeming comfort to the uncomfortable part of the transformation journey.

Journalling helps you to navigate the "yellow, gooey, sticky mess". And I have never had a client who, once they have embraced the journalling practice, regretted it.

“In the change from being a caterpillar to a butterfly, you are nothing more than **a yellow, gooey, sticky mess.**”

—TED FORBES

If you find journalling difficult in the beginning, here are three journalling techniques with which to start experimenting:

- Free writing – pen to paper, without stopping and placing no limits on what and how much you write.
- Guided journalling – use prompts or something you have read or heard as a stimulus for reflection. For example, examine a favourite quote or affirmation – what it means to you and how it applies to your life. Each of the practices in this book has prompts to guide your journalling.
- Stream of Consciousness journalling – as soon as you awaken, start writing, literally dumping anything that's on your mind with no prompts or guides – it's just what's in the deepest part of you coming out.

In the beginning, you may wonder what to journal on. Here are some structured ways to journal:

1. GRATITUDE – write down three things you are grateful for each day. Making gratitude lists whenever you feel any lack in your life reminds you that there is still much for you to be grateful for. Sometimes it's the same three things as the day before, and that's okay too.
2. CLARITY – when you are puzzled or unsettled about something, let go of thinking and put pen to paper and see what emerges. Use your journal to work out challenging situations and problems. Explore in depth whatever you are

going through until you become clear on the options open to you.

3. CLEANSING – cleanse toxic emotions, people, or situations. Your journal is a place to vent, to dump your thoughts and emotions. Make your journalling graphic, with colourful, expressive language. You may even consider writing a letter to someone who is toxic in your life (but *don't send the letter)*.
4. FORGIVENESS – journalling who and what you need to forgive will bring a sense of release (NB: Forgiveness is our 5th Joy Practice).
5. VISUALISATION – write detailed descriptions of what you envision for your life, your day, a project, your organisation, your team.
6. INTENTIONS – like visualisation, but more short-term and to the point.
7. ACTION – write your "to-do" lists for the day, week, month, or special events such as projects and travel.
8. AFFIRMATIONS – write short sentences or phrases affirming the good you desire. Affirmations about work are particularly empowering as they transform your mindset positively and put you in the frame of mind to create the workplace to which you aspire.
9. MUSING – and sometimes, you just muse. Record your insights about . . . anything! It's like "shooting the breeze" with a good friend and can be very enjoyable and insightful.

This is how my blog started, and even today, many of my blog posts come from the musings in my journal.

Your journal is yours. That you write is less important than what you write.

Your journal is a mirror of your life that helps you to examine your past and present and create your desired future.

JOY PRACTICE:

- Make journalling a daily habit to which you devote at least 5 minutes/day – set a timer or commit to writing a page per day.
- Best practice is to journal in the morning to set up your day with intention, and in the evening to reflect on how it went.
- Have a special place for journalling, with your journal and pens at the ready. Make it easy for yourself.
- Always remember to place no limits on what you write – you do NOT need to share your journal, or reread what you wrote!
- If you are concerned about someone finding and reading your journal, consider using a nickname or an emoji to hide the identity of a person about whom you are writing.

Several decades ago, at one of his massive personal transformational events, I heard self-development expert, Tony Robbins, say, "A life worth living is a life worth recording". Your leadership journey is worth recording.

Your journal is yours. That you write is less **important than what you write**.

JOY JOURNALLING PROMPTS FOR REFLECTION:

- What does joy mean to me?
- What does my leading joyfully look like and feel like, and what would be the impact on those I lead?
- How am I being joyful in my leadership?
- What's stopping me from being more joyful?
- What's the #1 thing I am learning or noticing about myself right now?

. . . AND REMEMBER:

Joy needs space

Joy is a serious value proposition

Joy is a choice

1 The Practice of Reflection

2 The Practice of Grounding Your Day in Joy

3 The Practice of Silence

4 The Practice of Making Peace With Time

5 The Practice of Forgiveness

6 The Practice of Acceptance

7 The Practice of Asking for Help

8 The Practice of Celebration

ESSENTIAL PRACTICE #2:

GROUNDING YOUR DAY IN JOY

“I hold the
splendid daylight
in my hands,
inwardly grateful
for a lovely day
Thank you, Life”

—LITANY BY GEORGE CAMPBELL

2

"Don't freak out but yesterday I had to go to the emergency room. I was cutting open an avocado and the knife sawed straight into the wedge between my index and middle fingers. I could see my bone and blood was spurting everywhere. My roommate, Paulina, came downstairs just as I was about to faint. She called a taxi, and we went to hospital. Six stitches!"

This WhatsApp message greeted me one Monday morning some years ago. It was from my daughter, Victoria, who had moved to London the prior week to pursue her Master's degree. She knows me well . . . she knew I would freak out (which mother wouldn't?). But I didn't. To my amazement, my reaction was calm, philosophical even, so that I could reply:

"I love your roommates . . . exhale please . . . life will continue apace whether u rush or not."

For days, I wondered how I had been able to respond in this very atypical way. Then it dawned on me – over the previous six weeks, I had committed to a daily morning ritual that takes a good hour or so BEFORE I check my technology. It is me-time, when I take care of my body (yoga), mind (reading, journalling), and spirit (meditation). There are days when I awaken not feeling enthused about doing this practice, even whilst knowing that my day will be immeasurably better if I do. Those are the mornings when I press the snooze button and have a back and forth with myself about why this morning, and just this morning please-please-please, can I just skip my morning ritual? Thankfully, the wiser Marguerite wins in that moment: "Just go take your shower, Marguerite, and then you can check in on the state of the world." Inevitably, the shower takes me into my me-time zone, and I slide into the rest of the practice.

Having done my practice that Monday morning, I was ready for the world . . . and for Victoria's message, which had been sitting in my phone since 2.59 a.m. Toronto time. My daughter was alive, well, and cared for. What was there to freak out about? Nothing.

What does this have to do with leadership? EVERYTHING! Many successful leaders have a morning routine, or "hour of power" as it's sometimes labelled, during which they commit to preparing themselves to face the day and all that it may bring. The routines are varied – the gym, meditation, a run, yoga, reading, writing, or some combination of these. They have spent years honing their practice until it has become as habitual as brushing their teeth.

What I have gleaned from their reports, and my own experience, is this:

How you start your day makes all the difference in how the day proceeds.

You cannot change what happens, but you can determine your response, and you are better able to respond in a constructive, conscious and positive way if you start your morning with intention.

So, my question to you:

How do you start your day, and does it make you feel alive, energised, and ready for anything?

In my first book, *"Free and Laughing: Spiritual Insights in Everyday Moments"*, I wrote in the chapter entitled Pliés:

> *Every ballet class throughout the world, be it at the New York City Ballet, the Kirov in Russia, or my daughter's ballet class in Jamaica, starts with pliés. A plié is the movement of bending the knees while keeping the back straight. Every class starts with the basics. Every ballerina knows that to master ballet, you must master pliés. And that the work of mastering the plié never ends.*

Just as the ballerina begins every class with pliés, before you turn up to work, start your day by designing and doing your

How you start your day makes all the difference in **how the day proceeds**.

own unique and powerful Morning Ritual that prepares your mind, body, and spirit. It means that you choose joy in the wee hours of the morning when it's calm and quiet and you are alone. That joy will fuel you for the rest of the day, so that you are able to meet whatever your work, the people you work with, and life in general might throw at you that day. And . . . stuff will be thrown at you. Guaranteed. It's how you prepare to be the best you can be that will make the difference.

Here's how to create and consistently do a morning ritual that gets your Body, Mind, and Spirit primed for joy.

YOUR BODY:

You have been lying supine and somewhat still for a few hours. Ease into the day with gentle movement to get the oxygen flowing through your body and the stiffness out of your joints.

- DEEP BREATHING – there are many important benefits of breathing deeply, which most of us, in our busy lives, don't do. Deep breathing releases toxins that have accumulated while we sleep; it energises us by getting fresh air deeply into our bodies; it eases tension and helps us to relax. It's actually quite simple to breathe – our bodies do it automatically for us. What's challenging is to be aware of our breath. Here are a few techniques to try:
    - Breathe normally and listen to the sound of your inhale and exhale.

How do you start your day, and does it **make you feel alive, energised, and ready for anything**?

    - Place your hand gently on your abdomen and notice how it moves as you inhale and exhale.
    - Count your breath, being aware of the space between the inhale and exhale: Inhale for 4; hold for 2; exhale for 5; hold for 2.
- STRETCHING – this is a good time to do some gentle stretches and yoga poses to wake up the body.
- WALKING – walking briskly for even just a few minutes also gets your body moving. If you can, go outside and greet the sun. Even in Toronto, where I live, no matter the season and the weather, I go outside every morning to walk my dog. The fresh air, the sun, and of course my doggie's inevitable joy, amplify my joy.

NB: Make sure to check with your doctor first if you are new to exercise!

YOUR MIND:

Programming your mind with positive thoughts will help you resist the barrage of negativity that will likely be coming at you throughout the day. Do one or all of these simple techniques every morning:

- BE GRATEFUL – gratitude is the most powerful practice for living a life of joy. Write down at least three things you are grateful for.

- AFFIRM YOUR TRUTH – affirmations are positive statements of what you hold or would like to hold to be true. They should be brief, in the present tense, and personal to you – start with "I" or "My". Keep trying them until you find a few that truly inspire you. Repeat them until they become true for you.
- BE INSPIRED – the words of others open our minds to new and different ideas, perspectives, and vistas. There are many daily inspirational readings available in hard copy or on the internet that you can easily access to start your morning inspired.
- REFLECT – Get a journal and place it with a pen in your dedicated morning space so that you don't have to search for it in the morning. And remember – you don't ever have to show it to anyone.

YOUR SPIRIT:

For a few minutes, sit with eyes closed, spine erect. This is your time to take care of your spirit through prayer, meditation, or just sitting still and feeling your connection with all around you.

Meditation is a powerful practice for retraining our minds. It brings our attention to a focal point and facilitates our having an open, accepting, non-reactive relationship with that focal point, where there are no thoughts about it, but simply the experience of it. It is not about having no thoughts; the mind is just doing what the mind was made to do: think. It's about retraining our attention. There are many different meditation techniques – for example, contemplative meditations that ask us to engage with a particular thought, and some that use sounds like chanting, mantras, or affirmations. There are silent meditations and guided meditations. What they have in common is a conscious choice to be fully present with focussed attention. I encourage you to choose one, develop a daily practice, and then explore other forms. Do what feels right for you.

PLAN B:

There will be times when you wake up late or have an early start that day. You may be tempted to skip your morning ritual. Create a contingency plan for this by designing an abridged version. For example, here's a 6-minute morning ritual you can do:

- Body – breathe and stretch for 2 minutes
- Mind – journal three things you are grateful for, and then affirm that this day will be joyful
- Spirit – sit, close your eyes, and be still for 2 minutes.

NOTE WELL: Do all this before you check your technology device.

As little as
6 minutes
can prepare
you to be
joyful
throughout
your day.

NOTE WELL:

Do all this before you check your technology device

Texts, e-mail, social media, the news – all can wait a few minutes until you are ready.

JOY PRACTICE:

1. Commit to your Morning Ritual as the most important thing to do, the minute you awaken, no matter how "late" you wake up.
2. Design your Morning Ritual for Body, Mind, and Spirit. I suggest writing it down and placing it in a conspicuous place, e.g. your bathroom mirror, where you will see it first thing in the morning.

3. Have an abbreviated version of your practice just in case you are short of time – the point is to do something, no matter how brief, to start your day with intention and attention.
4. Decide on the first step that sets your process in motion, as sometimes the prospect of an hour is just too much to consider in your state of grogginess. But you can at least convince yourself to take that first step.
5. Remove your technology device from your room the night before. I charge my phone in my home office, so even if I feel to, I can't roll over and check it. Get a good, old-fashioned alarm clock for your nightstand to replace your phone.
6. Time your process and set your alarm to awaken you in time for you to complete it. Over time, your body will adjust to the earlier time, and you may even find that an alarm is no longer needed.
7. DO IT, NO MATTER WHAT!

Now you are ready for the day – to check your emails, the news, the stock market, and to lead your team from a place of power, of strength, of joy. And if there's bad news or some challenge for you to address, you will be ready and energised to do so. As I did, after responding to Victoria's message. I purchased an avocado slicer for her.

JOY JOURNALLING PROMPTS FOR GROUNDING YOUR DAY:

Here are five prompts to get you started with your morning journal:

- How am I feeling this morning? What emotions are coming up for me?
- What am I grateful for right now?
- What's most on my mind as I face the day?
- What's working or not working in my Morning Ritual to bring me to a place of joy?
- What's my intention for today?

. . . AND REMEMBER:

Joy needs space

Joy is a serious value proposition

Joy is a choice

1 The Practice of Reflection

2 The Practice of Grounding Your Day in Joy

3 The Practice of Silence

4 The Practice of Making Peace With Time

5 The Practice of Forgiveness

6 The Practice of Acceptance

7 The Practice of Asking for Help

8 The Practice of Celebration

ESSENTIAL PRACTICE #3:

SILENCE

“The silence between the notes is what **creates the music.**”

—UNKNOWN

3

A coaching client shared with me, some three years after our coaching, that he had decided NOT to "shoot off an email" to someone who had upset him, remembering our coaching sessions about space for silence. He had chosen to say and do nothing, to be silent in that moment. And he was so happy that he had taken that approach, as subsequent events proved.

Silence is a spiritual practice of most religions. It is exhorted as a state of being where one taps into inner wisdom. Those who regularly practice silence can attest to its calming and life-affirming effects. Yet, in the hurly-burly, breakneck speed of business, silence does not seem to be appreciated. The voice is valued since opinions are what matter. Our silence may suggest that we have nothing to say, no point of view or position to stand

Sometimes the
best option is
to **say or do . . .**
nothing, to
choose silence
in word and
in deed.

for, or may even be viewed as a sign of weakness. We worry that others might conclude that we add little value. In meetings, silence is often considered space to be filled very quickly. As a workshop facilitator, I have observed silence being intercepted by someone raising a topic totally unrelated to the discussion, just to fill the gap. I have had CEOs express concern that "so-and-so" did not speak, even though I observed them actively listening and participating. And perhaps you have a team member who says very little, but every now and then, they share a few words that turn out to be very well-timed wisdom.

Sometimes the best option is to say or do . . . nothing, to choose silence in word and in deed.

Consider the hundreds of half-written social media comments that you may have erased mid-sentence, the LinkedIn comments that didn't get written, the telephone calls you didn't make, or the conversations you didn't have. These simple acts notwithstanding, the decision process one goes through when choosing silence might involve a range of emotions – anger at the person or situation, guilt at your lack of courage in copping out and not saying anything, frustration at seeing the person digging themselves deeper into their hole, betrayal – what type of friend/leader/boss/family member was I to say nothing? But then, peace. Because saying nothing was doing SOMETHING, an active step, a choice that you made consciously. You could so easily have lashed out, dashed off a response, or hit out in anger. Instead, you looked at the options and decided that saying nothing was the best one, in that moment.

Is it time to rethink silence in our leadership? How can we use silence in a positive way? Can it be of value to leaders and their teams? Silence can be a very powerful tool for communication and can be used very effectively by leaders, as it:

1. Allows us to truly listen. We cannot listen if we are speaking. Choosing to be silent means that we focus totally on what the other person is saying, rather than be thinking about the next thing we plan to say. Then, when they are finished, we remain silent before composing our response, if any is needed.
2. Garners wider participation. Often, when we choose to be silent, someone else will fill the space, thus allowing for the participation of others in your team. Someone will always break the silence, and it does not have to be you.
3. Allows you to gather your composure in difficult situations. Silence gives you space and time to choose your words carefully and then to make a response from a place of power.
4. Surfaces the unspoken. Often, the words we speak and our body language are out of sync, leading to confusion and distrust. Silencing our voice may clarify our message. Our bodies can still convey leadership; for example, by standing or sitting straight and making eye contact, we convey that

our silence is not an indicator of weakness, but of great strength.

Silence is more than not speaking.

Choosing to say or do nothing in the moment does not mean that you never say anything – there is time enough to say something, but later, at another time, if you so choose.

Let's explore the practice of silence beyond not speaking.

We live in a time of an abundance of technology that promised to make our lives easier, more productive, and even more joyful. But it hasn't worked out that way. Technology has cluttered our lives and work. Because it changes so fast, we are constantly on a quest for easier, faster, better; which leads to a flood of technology, causing confusion and stress. It's time to stop and put technology in perspective:

Technology is a TOOL, for our conscious and intentional use to make our lives easier and more joyful. We need space between us and technology.

We can practice silencing our technology in two areas that have become insidious in our work, and indeed our entire lives: the smartphone and emails.

Silence is more than **not speaking**.

Technology is
a TOOL, for our
conscious and
intentional use
to make our
lives easier
and more joyful.
**We need space
between us and
technology.**

THE SMARTPHONE

The smartphone is smart, but only if we use it smartly, as the tool it was meant to be, to serve and support us. Think of the myriad ways in which we use our phones. We literally can't leave home without them. And woe be unto us if we run out of power – we can't board the plane, we can't order the Uber, we can't pay for an item, we cannot check our emails, texts, and social media, and last but by no means least, we cannot make a phone call. Our smartphones are turned on 24/7 and have become intertwined with our very being.

There is diminishing space between us and our smartphones.

Silencing the phone opens the space for leading with joy. Must we answer every call or text the moment it comes in? Not at all – it's a conscious choice that allows us to remain present, for example, when speaking with a team member. The beauty of smartphones is that we know who is calling, so we can always call back. Do we have to check our phones the moment we awaken? NO! Your phone has been silent to you as you slept – extend that silence for an hour or two while you prepare for your day. The world can wait.

There is diminishing space between us and our smartphones.

Silencing the phone opens the space for **leading with joy**.

EMAILS

Jerome is a very busy executive at a leading academic institution. In our second coaching call, I asked him to track how he spent his time over three days. Here's what he found:

He was spending three hours PER DAY on emails!

Whilst he was surprised, I was not. I regularly see this with my coaching clients, and indeed, that used to be me. It's so easy to get trapped in the endless cycle of checking and responding to emails, spending hours each day wading through your inbox. You get to the end of the day, only to realise that the critical strategic work that leaders must do has not been touched. So, you put that off for another day, or work 2 or 3 extra hours well into the night. You are in email jail.

And email jail is very noisy and cluttered.

The allure of the seeming ease of email has made it an indispensable tool in our modern workplace, and indeed in all areas of our lives. However, this convenience comes at a cost:

- It drains our energy and increases stress, as we get caught up in minutiae and the demands of others.
- It reduces our productivity and ability to deliver on time.
- It disrupts our concentration, particularly if we have notifications on. This impedes our ability to focus on important projects and strategic initiatives.
- It makes us reactive rather than proactive about our work, leading to frustration.

- And it leaves little space for deep thinking, creativity, and innovation, which is so necessary in these fast-paced, ever-changing times!

Believe it or not, we can silence our emails by setting boundaries, without apology. Establish designated times throughout the day to check and respond to emails, rather than allowing them to dictate your schedule. Resist the temptation to check emails outside of those hours – revel in the silence, as uncomfortable as it may feel when you start the practice. If that's difficult for you, take emails off your phone and check only on your computer. There's no need to apologise for establishing your boundaries, as your intention is to become more efficient and effective, and thus better able to serve others, including those who are emailing you. And you set the example for your team members to get out of their own email jail. Try going further with an email holiday once per week or month. For that day, do not check your emails. It's that simple.

Smartphones and email are great tools, but like all tools, they only work if you use them appropriately and not allow them to use you. Choose to silence your technology, just as you may choose to be silent in a conversation.

JOY PRACTICE

Spend time every day, and throughout the day, even for a few minutes, in your own silence, listening to the wisdom of your inner voice. Notice your emotions, without judgement. Breathe and get calm.

Reduce how much you speak and allow others to speak. You have two ears and one mouth for a reason – to listen twice as much as you speak. When someone speaks, resist the temptation to respond immediately. First, listen, and then take a moment of silence before you respond, and only if necessary. Think about what you want to accomplish by your response. Consider your options for responding, remembering that saying and doing nothing is also an option. Tune into what the other person is saying. Being silent is more than not talking. Have you ever been in a conversation with someone who was not talking, yet you knew they weren't listening to you? They seemed far away, consumed by the noise and distraction in their heads. You saw in their eyes a distant gaze that said: "I am not into you at this moment. I am not listening". Put down your phone, make eye contact, and show whoever you are communicating with that they are the only one that matters to you right now. Listen with your eyes, ears, mind, and heart.

Take technology breaks throughout the day. Deliberately silence your smartphone and emails in the morning.

Establish a ground rule in all meetings, including virtual meetings, of not checking emails or using phones.

Go places without your phone – the boardroom, to one-on-one meetings with team members and clients, and yes, the washroom. Observe the difference it makes in how you feel and act, and the impact on others.

Thoughtful use of silence by leaders can create the space for harmony and joy in our workplaces. Sit quietly, silence technology, and open the workplace for joy.

JOY JOURNALLING PROMPTS FOR SILENCE:

- Reflecting on recent conversations, where could I have practiced being silent?
- What challenges am I experiencing in holding silence?
- How are others responding to my silence?
- Am I using my smartphone, or is it using me?
- How am I doing in getting out of email jail?

. . . AND REMEMBER:

Joy needs space

Joy is a serious value proposition

Joy is a choice

Thoughtful use of silence by leaders can create the space for harmony and joy in our workplaces. **Sit quietly, silence technology, and open the workplace for joy.**

1 The Practice of Reflection

2 The Practice of Grounding Your Day in Joy

3 The Practice of Silence

4 The Practice of Making Peace With Time

5 The Practice of Forgiveness

6 The Practice of Acceptance

7 The Practice of Asking for Help

8 The Practice of Celebration

ESSENTIAL
PRACTICE #4:

MAKING PEACE WITH TIME

“Your time is limited, **so don’t waste it living someone else’s life**.”

—STEVE JOBS

4

I will never forget you saying to me, "If you are late, you are late." Kendrick, a longtime coaching client who is a partner at a large global consulting firm, chuckled as he shared a few things that had made a big difference in his work. We had worked tirelessly on Kendrick's relationship with time, and its impact on his stress level (off the charts), his leadership, and his happiness. Kendrick had now cultivated the habit of stopping to meditate and to find a moment of calm, no matter how late he was, instead of rushing out the door each morning. He had made peace with time.

The scarcest resource that a leader must manage is time, his or her own, and the time of others.

The workplace is driven by time. There are specific hours for starting and ending the workday and for taking breaks, with

The scarcest resource that a leader must manage is time, **his or her own, and the time of others**.

some employees required to clock in and out. Woe be unto us if we are late.

We complain that we don't have time for this or that, that we've run out of time, or that we need more time.

We have specific times for meetings to start, although ending times seem to be open, resulting in meetings dragging on way "over time".

We have deadlines. Ever wonder why they are called "deadlines" and not termed something like "lifelines", "success-lines", or "completion-lines"? Or even better, "JOYLINES"?

The experience of working from home during the COVID-19 pandemic made many of us think we would have more time. After all, we didn't have to dress for work, nor commute to and fro', and no-one was popping into our office for a casual chat, nor a water cooler at which to hang out. But most of us seemed to be even more time-strapped than ever. And this has continued unabated with our post-pandemic return to the office.

We try everything to control time and to get more of it. We attend time management courses, read books, schedule our calendars, download apps, set timers, start work early, and stay late – all to no avail. It seems that the more we try to manage time, the more it manages us.

The problem is not time; it's that we are at war with it.

Can we really manage time? Can we manage something that is totally outside of our control, which ticks on no matter what, and will continue long after we are gone? Can we make more

The problem
is not time;
**it's that
we are at
war with it**.

Perhaps
it's time to
**make peace
with time**.

of something that is given in equal measure to each of us in terms of hours in the day, minutes in the hour, and seconds in the minute? It's not possible. Why fight a battle that we cannot win?

Perhaps it's time to make peace with time.

(Many thanks to Lama Surya Das for this insight in his book "*Buddha Standard Time*").

How do we do this?

By slowing down, being early, and choosing to say NO!

SLOW DOWN

Until recently, I thought that I would slow down, take things easier, and be more orderly after I had completed everything on my to-do list. But there has rarely been a day, week, or month when I managed to accomplish it all. Time always conquered my list, leaving my life as collateral damage. This was unsustainable and hardly joyful. So, I stopped my relentless focus on getting everything done, realising that time would stop me if I didn't change my relationship with it. I slowed down.

When we slow down, we open space for our priorities to become clear, allowing our energy to flow to these priorities with ease so that they get done. Then, time feels like what it really is – endless. However, if we are not clear about our priorities, this space that we open may be filled with unwanted, unproductive activities.

There are 24 hours in each day. By our actions, we consciously or unconsciously choose how we spend our time. The more aware and honest we are about our busyness, the greater will be our ability to focus on our priorities and get the important work done.

The third habit in the classic bestseller, *The 7 Habits of Highly Effective People,* by Stephen Covey, is:

Prioritise by putting first things first.

In his book *First Things First,* Covey outlines the Priority Management Matrix, a tool that my coaching clients report is the single most transformative tool I share. In this matrix, Covey identifies two dimensions:

- Urgency – Tasks requiring immediate action or attention.
- Importance – Tasks with high significance and value to goals.

He invites us to view all our tasks using a simple four-quadrant matrix that plots Urgency and Importance. Every task fits one of these quadrants:

1. QUADRANT 1: Urgent and important tasks such as crises, pressing problems, and deadline-driven projects. This is the quadrant of **DEMAND**, which often leads to stress and burnout.
2. QUADRANT 2: Not urgent, but important. This is the heart of effective leadership, signified by tasks that focus

Prioritise by putting **first things first.**

on planning, prevention, developing new opportunities, and building relationships. Proactive in nature, it is the quadrant of **FULFILLMENT**. This is the quadrant of "first things first". Be aware that tasks in this quadrant are easy to overlook or delay as they are not (yet) pressing. Over time, they may end up in Quadrant #1 due to procrastination. Be patient, take your time, and slowly move more and more tasks into fulfilment – and do them!

3. QUADRANT 3: Urgent, but not important tasks such as telephone calls, attending to interruptions, and the demands from other people. This is the quadrant of **DELUSION** in which urgency may be conflated with importance.
4. QUADRANT 4: Not urgent and not important – Trivia, busywork, time-wasting activities such as social media scrolling. This is the quadrant of **DISTRACTION**.

Ask yourself:

"In which quadrant am I spending most of my time?"

It's quite common that at the start of our coaching, my clients report spending over 50% of their time in the Demand and Delusion quadrants, i.e. in a state of urgency. Our coaching agenda becomes clear – move more of their tasks to Fulfilment, resulting in a sense of calm and ease in their work and the joy of completing the work that matters.

Consciously choosing the tasks we must focus on each day is the key not just to efficiency (doing more things faster), but more importantly, effectiveness, i.e., doing the things that will generate the results we desire. Our first thing should be to identify our priorities, and as much as possible, replace urgency with importance. Note that we will always have tasks in each quadrant. The question is: do they get there by default or by design?

BE EARLY:

Making peace with time requires that we consciously and deliberately create space in our day.

What does "on time" mean to you?

One version is to get to one's destination on the dot, which is really "just in time." We may seem composed and confident on the outside, but feel stressed and in turmoil on the inside.

Making peace
with time
requires
that we
**consciously
and deliberately
create space
in our day.**

Another approach is to arrive early. When we do this, we will be calm, cool, and collected, feeling relaxed and prepared, and looking very competent and professional to those who arrive after. What can we do to arrive early, and in a state of ease, grace, and joy? There's the usual stuff: preparation such as packing our bags and choosing our outfit the night before, getting up early, leaving home 15 minutes early, not over scheduling the day, and so on. Those are the things we know we are supposed to do, and IF we do them, we should be early, or at the very least, be on time. But I have some additional tricks that work for me:

- Schedule transfer time – when scheduling appointments, allow extra time for moving, whether walking, by public transport, or by car. Coming from a manufacturing background and having had experience with time and motion studies, I am very aware of how not including or miscalculating transfer time (i.e. the time in between processes) can throw total processing time out of whack. It is the same with getting somewhere early – I must factor in walking to the subway, buying tickets, going down the escalator, and then, if I have to transfer to another train, time to move from one to another. Plus, walking time from arrival at the destination, up the elevator, to the receptionist, and to the actual meeting room. It all adds up, and so you must budget for transfer time.

- Add 15 minutes to the estimated time. Why? Because stuff happens! A tip I learned from my sister is – never schedule to leave on the quarter hour. Inevitably, you will leave on the hour or half-hour, as if your brain can't compute 15-minute intervals. Time has proven her right.
- Keep a stash of articles to read or podcasts to listen to. When you are heading out, simply take one or two with you to read as you wait. This way, you don't view waiting time as wasted time. It becomes productive time that you might even look forward to.

There is one other big thing I have learned that helps me to be early – saying "NO" to requests that will interrupt my schedule. For example, no squeezing in a phone call with someone 5 minutes before I am heading out the door, or trying to fit just one more appointment or meeting into the day. Say "NO" and schedule at another time. Most things can wait. There are very few real emergencies.

CHOOSE TO SAY **NO**

"Look at my week, Marguerite!"

Daniel had indicated before our fortnightly coaching call that foremost on his mind were the endless meetings that cluttered his days. He was feeling overwhelmed, time-strapped, and frustrated at not being able to devote the time necessary to close important deals for his company.

I asked him to share his calendar for that week on the ZOOM screen. "A picture paints a thousand words" was never truer. I immediately saw Daniel's predicament – his days were chock-full of meetings, resulting in him working until 11.00 p.m. many nights. And STILL he was unable to get his work done.

So, we got to work on a Calendar Clearing exercise. Starting on Monday of the following week, we went through each meeting in his calendar, exploring a series of questions:

1. Do you have to attend this meeting?
2. Why is it important for you to be there? Is this the best use of your time?
3. If you must attend, do you have to attend it for the entire duration?
4. If you don't have to be there for the entire duration, how much time will you devote to it?
5. If you don't have to attend the meeting at all, is there someone who could represent you? This could be an opportunity to develop a key member of your team by

exposing them to broader opportunities and for them to expand their scope.

6. If you will not be attending the meeting, decline the invitation so that you get it out of your calendar.

By the end of the exercise, Daniel was in disbelief – he had one afternoon and a whole day void of meetings!

Does this scenario sound familiar? To climb the ladder of success, expand our profile, and grow our leadership trajectory, we feel compelled to say "yes" to everything – yes to opportunities that stretch us, yes to working late, yes to taking on someone else's incomplete job. I could go on. Indeed, many of us live in "YES" as a default state.

But sometimes being in perpetual YES-mode stretches us too far, to a point that is detrimental to our own well-being.

Everything we do is a yes to something and a no to something else.

Saying "Yes" to something means you are saying "No" to other things (and vice versa). Explore the opposite of your default.

It's important to put space between whatever you are asked to do and your actual response. Be aware of your default response – mine is typically "yes"; for others, it's "no". Know what makes you likely to respond the way you do: what are your underlying values, beliefs, and assumptions? What experiences have validated your usual response? Are these still valid? How well are they working for you?

Everything we do is a yes to something and a **no to something else**.

Remember that for every request, there are three basic responses:

Yes

No

Maybe

"Maybe" is a great response to give you the space to think before responding. Be aware, however, that "maybe", if delayed too long, may be interpreted as procrastination, indecisiveness, and an inability to decide. You run the risk of ceding your power to someone else, who may decide for you.

Whilst you are pondering the pros and cons of your responses, pay attention to the signals you are getting from your body, emotions, and mental state. Feelings of being overwhelmed, tension in your body, and the lack of mental clarity are signals that something is not sitting well with you. Listen to your gut!

It's also important to remember that whatever decision you have made, you can choose to change it. There will always be opportunities. We do not have to say "Yes" to everyone and everything that comes our way. We have full power and ability to choose how we spend our precious time.

JOY PRACTICE:

Each morning, scan your "to do" list and identify the ONE most important thing you intend to accomplish on that day. Do it mindfully and with focus, and take a moment to congratulate

Remember that for every request, there are three basic responses:

Yes

No

Maybe

yourself when it's done. Then you can tackle the next item, and the next, one by one. In no time, you will have completed, if not all the items on your list, at least the most important. What a great use of your time! If there are interruptions (and there will be), attend to them and then RETURN TO YOUR PRIORITY NUMBER ONE.

Plan to be early for everything. Reconfigure your appointments to make sure you are early for every meeting. Factor in transfer time and budget an extra 15 minutes for your departure. Schedule at least 15 minutes between virtual meetings – i.e. no "hardstop" to end one meeting and start another at the same time! What's the worst that can happen? Maybe you won't be early . . . but you will probably be just in time.

Accept that if you are late, you are late. Don't rush. Slow down and get wherever you are going calmly and "in due time". Ever notice that when you rush to be on time, you only save a few minutes, even seconds? Slow down and be late. Just make sure to call and inform other attendees that you are running late, and of course, apologise when you arrive. And while you are observing your lateness, reflect on why and what you can do to make sure it doesn't happen the next time.

Get comfortable with saying "NO". No need for an apology or for a long explanation. Just a calm, confident "NO". Practice in front of a mirror until you FEEL comfortable.

Every human is equal in this regard – we all get 24 hours in each day. The difference is what we each choose to do with those 24 hours.

JOY JOURNALLING PROMPTS FOR MAKING PEACE WITH TIME:

- What's my relationship with time?
- How well am I focussing on my priorities?
- Am I paying sufficient attention to other areas of my life?
- What am I learning about myself and how I am spending my time?

. . . AND REMEMBER:

Joy needs space

Joy is a serious value proposition

Joy is a choice

Every human is equal in this regard – we all get 24 hours in each day. The difference is **what we each choose to do with those 24 hours**.

ESSENTIAL PRACTICE #5:

FORGIVENESS

"To **forgive**
is to set a
prisoner free
and discover
that the
prisoner
was you."

—ARCHBISHOP DESMOND TUTU

5

During the coffee break in a workshop a few years ago, Megan, a member of the management team and a workshop participant, asked if she could have a quiet word with me. Two years prior, she had applied for a position in the company and was passed over for someone else. She had heard through the grapevine that she was the best candidate, but was never given any explanation why she had not gotten the job. I could see the pain on Megan's face. She was angry at the management of the company, and it was literally eating away at her. I was not surprised when she told me that she was suffering from a serious illness. I coached her as best as I could in the few minutes and urged her to let go of the anger towards those whom she felt had wronged her. I invited her to forgive them.

The solution to the pain is forgiveness, which has its place at work just as much as in our personal lives.

Megan is not alone.

In the work I do with leaders and their teams, I see a lot of pain – people who work hard, qualify themselves, achieve results, and yet are passed over for promotion; the pain of being terminated after years of hard work, sacrifice and loyalty to the organisation; the pain of people hurt by insensitive and abusive bosses and co-workers. People suffer in silence. But their actions speak loudly. They withdraw, they resist, and they work at the minimum. Their pain is toxic, affecting productivity, customer service, and profitability. It permeates the organisational culture and perpetuates itself, spreading beyond those who feel wronged. It stifles joy.

Think about the trajectory of your career and the situations that caused you pain. Remember the supervisor who refused to move your performance appraisal score from 3.9 to 4.0 and so cost you a sizeable bonus? How about that "boss from hell" who yelled at you in front of the entire department and made you feel smaller than the bug scurrying along the floor? And then there's that team member you supervised who went behind your back, directly to your boss's boss to report you. There are likely numerous people who have done you wrong (or so you continue to believe). The experiences happened years ago, yet they still hurt.

The solution to the pain is forgiveness, which has its place at work just as much as in our personal lives.

I used to think that forgiveness was about letting others off the hook. I thought it meant telling someone that I forgave them. I thought it was something I proffered magnanimously to others, ensconced in my rightness. I thought it was something that I doled out like tablespoons of water to someone dying of thirst. They would be so grateful for my benevolence, and I would feel so . . . well, so righteous.

"Forgiveness is a selfish act that frees you from being controlled by the past."

This quote that I came across many years ago was a life-changer. It made me realise that forgiveness was not about the other person, but about me. Since then, I have dedicated time and effort to forgiveness in copious and unimpeded amounts, in all aspects of my life, including my work. Retreats, workshops, books, journalling, coaching, counselling, and therapy, Archbishop Tutu's Forgiveness Challenge – I have done them and done them again, and again. Some people I have forgiven seventy times seven, as Jesus advised the Apostle Peter, who had asked how many times he should forgive. Yet things kept coming up. It seemed like forgiveness was the proverbial onion – I peeled the layers, and peeled and peeled and peeled some more. Yet still there were blockages in my life, and lack of forgiveness kept resurfacing. I was peeling onions by the bushel, and it was very uncomfortable.

I came to realise that there's another aspect that is important in forgiveness:

Release the need to be right.

This presents a conundrum for leaders, whose primary function is to get things right. Leadership requires visionary

"Forgiveness is a selfish act that **frees you from being controlled by the past.**"

—UNKNOWN

thinking, the ability to imagine and articulate futures that others might not yet see, and the resilience and fortitude to take their team into uncharted territory. Leaders are therefore rewarded for being decisive, for taking action, and solving problems. This requires taking positions that might be opposed by others. To get things done, to achieve the results expected, especially during these uncertain and rapidly changing times, leaders may think and say that they have the answer, that they have no time for the opinions of others, that they cannot wait. "My way or the highway". After all, what are leaders rewarded for, if not for being right?

But getting things right does not mean being right, at least not all the time. Much of the pain we see at the workplace is due to one or both sides digging into their "rightness", and neither yielding. It is the leader's responsibility to break the gridlock and give up being right, to choose, as Tony Robbins said, "to be happy or to be right. But you can't be both".

Release the need to be right.

As I journalled one morning, this thought came to me: "Whenever I have any negative thought, no matter how minute, it means there is something to forgive, something to release." I have numerous negative thoughts each day, so I certainly have many opportunities to forgive. Rather than tackling forgiveness as a massive, one-time event, I decided to add forgiveness as a morning journalling practice.

Here's what I now do:

- I write in my journal: "Right here and right now I forgive."
- And then I sit in silence and observe what comes up. Typically, a name or an experience will surface – it may be someone close to me, a stranger who barged ahead of me in the subway the day before, a client, or a potential client who turned down my proposal.
- Then I write. I acknowledge the negative thoughts, writing extensively until I can find no more negatives. I explore situations in which I felt I was right, the impact this had, and what giving up my rightness would mean. Once finished, I continue: "I now forgive and release."
- If no one comes up, then I write: "I forgive anyone for whom I hold a negative thought." This is my forgiveness insurance – just in case there's anything at all that is lurking in my subconscious.
- But there's always another person to be forgiven – myself. Somehow it always comes around to this: "I forgive myself."

> Yes, the seventy times seven and more applies to me. At the minimum, I forgive myself for holding the negative thought. Many times, there's another bout of venting and release, until I feel empty and clear.

Upon completion, I feel light – I am free from the control of the past – at least until the next negative thought.

JOY PRACTICE:

Today, start the process of forgiving the people in your work life for whom you hold any negative thoughts, no matter how minor or irrational that thought may seem. Do this every day until one day you awaken, and you get to this point, like my friend Maxine shared: "I know that I have forgiven someone when I think about them and I can smile from my heart about them. It truly is a process."

And always remember that the NUMBER ONE person to forgive is yourself – the times when you were the "boss from hell", when you gave a low performance rating, when you lost your temper and yelled at someone, and so on. Carry those experiences with you no more, so that you can put your energy into leading the people in your organisation to achieve their very best.

JOY JOURNALLING PROMPTS ON FORGIVENESS:

- Who do I need to forgive today?
- What do I need to forgive myself for?
- What do I believe I am absolutely right about? Why? Suppose I am wrong?

. . . AND REMEMBER:

Joy needs space

Joy is a serious value proposition

Joy is a choice

1 The Practice of Reflection

2 The Practice of Grounding Your Day in Joy

3 The Practice of Silence

4 The Practice of Making Peace With Time

5 The Practice of Forgiveness

6 The Practice of Acceptance

7 The Practice of Asking for Help

8 The Practice of Celebration

ESSENTIAL PRACTICE #6:

ACCEPTANCE

“If I accept the sunshine and warmth, then **I must also accept the thunder and lightning.**”

—KAHLIL GIBRAN

6

"Ah so she stay."

Celia, a high-potential executive leadership coaching client, had requested an urgent call with me for help on how to deal with a particularly difficult team member at work. The person's behaviour was causing her great angst, to the point of physical symptoms of stress. On hearing the description of the behavioural history of the angst-causing person, I shared the Jamaican saying – "Ah so she stay" (meaning: "That's just how she is"). You will hear Jamaicans say this with a sense of acceptance and little emotion or angst. It's often accompanied by a dismissive swivel of the body, a shrug of the shoulder, and a wave of the hand.

"Ah so she stay" harkens to a very important step in moving forward in relationships, which is about accepting other people's actions. Many find the practice of acceptance difficult as they view it as condoning or approving of the action. It is not. Some actions are too hurtful to consider "acceptance" in the typical usage of the word. What you are accepting is that the action happened. It took place. For some, a more palatable word may be "acknowledgement," which means that you notice the action, with as little emotion and judgement as possible, as if you are watching a play or a movie.

In this way, you recognise that the person's behaviour is about them, not you, and there's not much you can do about it in that moment. That's where "Ah so she stay" is useful, to remind oneself that the person is just that way. I find that taking this approach reduces my own angst and allows me the space to consider and decide on my response, rather than submit to a knee-jerk reaction, which rarely ends well.

Once Celia embraced the "Ah so she stay" philosophy, we completed the session with an action plan for each time she felt the person had pushed her buttons. I could feel her frustration and distress dissipating, as her mood lightened and she could see a way out. She had taken back her power.

Acceptance is not passive, nor weak.

Are there people at your workplace who display negative behaviour that upsets and frustrates you? Of course there are! They may be your peers, persons who report directly to you, your boss, suppliers, and even customers. You must work with

Acceptance is not passive, nor weak.

them, so it behoves you to do your very best to address the situation by first accepting it as it is.

But what, after acceptance, should be done to address behaviours that must be addressed? For that is your function in leading your team – to create and ensure a culture that is positive, uplifting, and in sync with the core values of the organisation. You can't allow dysfunctional behaviour to continue.

Acceptance lays the foundation for a different type of conversation. Instead of "But you cannot do this" or, "You have to change", you open up to the give-and-take of exploring the behaviour, the impact it had, and what the person can do differently in the future. This is less about you speaking and more about asking questions and listening as your team member engages in his/her own self-reflection. The behaviour will change only when the person decides to change. You cannot do it for them, but you can help them do it for themselves.

"**Acceptance** doesn't mean resignation; it means understanding that something is what it is **and that there's got to be a way through it.**"

—MICHAEL J. FOX

In this type of conversation, it is important to start with the "Ah so she stay" behaviour, i.e., what you observed and accepted happened. This releases the judgement you may feel, as it is a simple statement of fact:

"I observed . . . "

You can then move on to share your observation of the impact that it had on others, including you. Again, in a matter-of-fact, non-judgemental way. And now the pivot conversation – asking questions such as:

"How do you feel about this situation and the impact on you and others?"

"What would you have preferred to happen?"

"What could you have done differently?"

"What do you commit to doing in the future?"

"How can I help you?"

Throughout this, your job is to listen as the other person struggles with deepening introspection. This is not the time for you to give answers!

JOY PRACTICE:

Learn to get comfortable with acceptance:

1. Observe dispassionately. Notice the other person's behaviour – just what you observe, not what you interpret

the behaviour to be, nor the person's intentions. And notice your own emotions, with no judgement. Accept that what you feel, you feel.

2. Accept that you cannot change the person (remind yourself how difficult it is to change your own behaviour).
3. Consider your options and decide on your response, knowing that you have total power over the way you choose to respond.

At work, there's a job to be done, clients to serve, sales to be made, and objectives to be met. You must choose a response that will enable you to do your best work, signal to the person that the behaviour is not appropriate, and move the relationship to a positive footing. You are in a much better position to do this when you have accepted the person and the situation.

Many find the practice of acceptance difficult as they view it as condoning or approving of the action. **It is not.**

JOY JOURNALLING PROMPTS FOR ACCEPTANCE:

- Who am I disagreeing or fighting with?
- What aspect of their behaviour do I disagree with?
- What might happen if I simply accept them just as they are?

. . . AND REMEMBER:

Joy needs space

Joy is a serious value proposition

Joy is a choice

1 The Practice of Reflection

2 The Practice of Grounding Your Day in Joy

3 The Practice of Silence

4 The Practice of Making Peace With Time

5 The Practice of Forgiveness

6 The Practice of Acceptance

7 The Practice of Asking for Help

8 The Practice of Celebration

ESSENTIAL PRACTICE #7:

ASKING FOR HELP

“Sometimes **asking for help is the bravest move you can make**. You don’t have to go it alone.”

—STEVE KEATING

7

5:00 a.m. on a cold, dark November morning in Nepal. Snowflakes fluttered to the ground, making the narrow path up the steep mountain that much more treacherous. We had started out at about 4,800m above sea level, the air at this altitude bereft of oxygen. Each step was an agonising, slow motion of gasping for air and feeling with my boot for the safety of the next step. A steady "clop clop clop" sound grew closer, revealing a string of horses wending their way up the mountain. What were they doing here? I wondered, as they trod past me. I couldn't help noticing the horses' certainty of exactly where to set their next hoof.

Nigel, my trekking partner, had been struggling even more than I. Suraj, our guide, approached me, wanting to know if I thought Nigel would accept a horse. I told him yes, and was gratified to see Nigel on horseback, relieved of some of his suffering.

I trekked on. Slower and slower, as the mountain got steeper. I was exhausted, cold, and every step was agony. Finally, at the next way-stop, I looked at the horses gathered, then to Suraj and said, "Please give me a horse". A quick negotiation on price, and the next thing I know, I was perched on a beautiful animal, with hooves as sure as if at one with the terrain. I was breathing calmly for the first time in 2 hours. My eyes were raised to the dawning sunrise of the magnificent Himalayas, and my heart was soaring with joy.

I had struggled with the decision to ask for help. Then, I remembered what my true goal was – to enjoy everything the Annapurna Circuit Trek had to offer, including going through the challenge of navigating the Thorang-La Pass at 5,416m above sea level. I looked at the situation and realised I had a choice – I could continue the agony of relying on my two legs or enjoy the trek atop my four-hoofed friend. I released bravado and ego, realising that it wouldn't matter to anyone that I took the "easy" way out. It wouldn't matter that I made a choice for myself that was in my best interest. I let go all thoughts of being a failure and made the choice to ask for help.

Somehow, we have got the idea that asking for help shows weakness. We fear being viewed as incompetent, unable to solve problems, and not being up to the task of leading. Basically, we fear being vulnerable. Note that these are thoughts raging only in our minds. And as with all thoughts, we have the power to change them – in a heartbeat.

Consider this:

Asking for help is another way to view delegation.

Contrary to common misconceptions, delegation is not about offloading burdens onto already overloaded shoulders. Instead, you can view it as a tool for unleashing potential and cultivating talent within your team, encouraging and empowering them to take on new, challenging tasks, and freeing you for the more strategic aspects of your job. It's about recognising and harnessing the unique strengths of each team member, aligning tasks with their competencies and providing opportunities for them to excel, thus allowing them to shine. These are lofty aspirations that begin with the leader opening space by asking for their help. When you approach delegation this way, your team members are often happy to oblige.

The benefits of asking for help are numerous, but here are a few:

- You release your stress and anxiety. No longer is the task yours alone.
- You model true teamwork – people can't work together without helping each other, and that means asking for help and receiving it graciously. When your team sees you asking for help, they will understand that it's safe for them to do so as well and to offer help to others.
- Your team members see the bigger picture, stretch, and grow as they take on tasks that you release.

Asking for help is **another way to view delegation.**

Asking yourself these four questions will enable you to seek, and receive the right help:

1. Does this task need to be done? Not all tasks are created equal, so you must discern what is essential. Be ruthless in your inquiry – is it a must-do, a like-to-do, or a who-cares task? Focus on the must-do. There's nothing more frustrating for a team member than being asked to help with a meaningless task.
2. If so, do I have to do it? Challenge your instinct to shoulder every task yourself. Your team members have brains and skills that you mightn't have.
3. If I don't, who is the best person to do it? This requires a deep understanding of each team member's strengths, preferences, and development goals in order to unearth

and leverage the skills and commitment of the best person for the task. Making your inquiry independent of job titles and organisational hierarchy can reveal hidden talents and provide opportunities for development deep within your team.

4. What support or guidance does the team member need? Providing ongoing monitoring and guidance, as well as the necessary resources, will ensure the success of the team member in executing the task and your success in getting it done without doing it yourself.

Mastering the art of asking for help can be a catalyst for unlocking the full potential of individuals and teams. By embracing a mindset of empowerment, you can harness the collective talents of your team, drive the right results, and allow flourishing and joy in your team.

Stop battling with yourself. Ask for help.

JOY PRACTICE:

As you go through your day, look for opportunities to ask for help. If you observe yourself stuck in a situation, feeling overwhelmed and drowning in the chaos, confusion, or hardship about a report or project, for example, STOP and:

1. REFOCUS: What's the goal? What am I trying to achieve, and most importantly, why?

2. REALIGN: Is what I am doing now moving me towards that goal with the momentum and focus required?
3. REQUEST: If not, where do I need help, and who can I ask?

And then ASK, even if you are scared out of your wits. Do it anyway. You might be surprised that people are more willing to help than you had thought, as you hear things like:

"I thought you'd never ask!"

"I'd be happy to help."

"What do you need me to do?"

Stop battling with yourself. **Ask for help.**

JOY JOURNALLING PROMPTS FOR ASKING FOR HELP:

- What did I do today that someone else could have done?
- What stopped me from asking for help?
- Who could have helped me?

. . . AND REMEMBER:

Joy needs space

Joy is a serious value proposition

Joy is a choice

1 The Practice of Reflection

2 The Practice of Grounding Your Day in Joy

3 The Practice of Silence

4 The Practice of Making Peace With Time

5 The Practice of Forgiveness

6 The Practice of Acceptance

7 The Practice of Asking for Help

8 The Practice of Celebration

ESSENTIAL PRACTICE #8:

CELEBRATION

“One love,
one heart.
Let’s get
together
**and feel
alright.**”

—BOB MARLEY

8

"So, what are you doing to celebrate"?

Even over ZOOM, I could read her quizzical look – "Celebrate? But they were just doing their job. It's what they are paid to do".

Jessica, a senior Finance Executive – my coaching client – had shared that during her vacation, her team had pulled out all stops to meet a critical timeline without disturbing her well-deserved time away from work. Our conversation before she departed had been about her having an unplugged vacation, i.e., not checking emails or her phone. She committed to trying, even as she expressed reservations that her team would get things done on their own. But they did, and she was touched and extremely proud of them.

One of the fundamental responsibilities of leading with joy is a commitment to helping your team win. **And winning requires celebration**.

In my experience working with leaders, there is a common view that because someone is paid to do something, there is no need to go the extra step of celebrating their achievement. Where does this belief that compensation and celebration are mutually exclusive come from? Are we not happy, joyful, and grateful when someone simply does what they are paid to do? Because when they don't, we sure are miserable.

One of the fundamental responsibilities of leading with joy is a commitment to helping your team win. And winning requires celebration.

How often do you celebrate at work? I don't mean the annual service awards shindig, or the once-in-a-while pizza party. I mean the spontaneous, no-holds-barred heralding and honouring of good deeds and accomplishments, no matter how large or small, and whether special or normal. Do you not celebrate birthdays, anniversaries, or special life achievements like new babies, graduations, or weddings? And don't you also celebrate your new sales rep closing his/her first sale? Or a compliment from a customer for a member of your team? A proposal accepted? Or a new client signed on? Or the achievement of a milestone towards reaching a target?

Celebration is important and powerful for several reasons:

1. It creates space in the workday, a little breath in the daily grind of work.
2. It demonstrates your caring and thoughtfulness.
3. It tells your team that their efforts are noticed and that they matter.

4. It shows appreciation and affirms the right things, so that your team becomes clearer on what is expected.
5. It lifts the energy of the entire team, not just the person or situation being celebrated.

Fundamentally, celebration shows that your team members are valued.

In my opinion, you can't have too much celebration! But there is a risk that it becomes routine and meaningless. So, for celebration to "work," it must be genuine, heartfelt, in the moment (or as close to the moment as possible), and in keeping with the sensibilities and preferences of those whom you are celebrating. It requires your presence in terms of being aware of moments when it's appropriate and helpful. You must be tuned into your team to notice and acknowledge instances of achievement and their own pride in their achievement. It also requires your sensitivity to what makes them tick, and therefore what's meaningful to them. Celebration is not about you and what you like. (I have learned that not everyone likes chocolate cake – my favourite way to celebrate).

Laughter is a big part of celebration.

Create a celebratory environment by bringing a sense of lightness and play to work, as serious as it is, with laughter. One of the most glorious sounds the human being makes is laughter. Have you ever noticed how good you feel when you laugh and when you hear others laugh? Even a smile starts to change your countenance. And a good "belly-laugh" literally shakes your entire body, creating space at the most cellular level. And notice how contagious laughter is. It is nigh impossible for someone to laugh, and for others not to start laughing too!

In Jamaica, you will hear someone say, "Hear dis now . . ." (Listen to this). This is a signal to stop what we are doing and gather around for the relating of some funny story, a different perspective on an experience, or a joke. For just a moment, we change our state and become present. "Hear this now" is really an invitation to "be here now". And in the moment of being present, you have created the space for celebration and joy.

A few days after our conversation, Jessica sent me a photo of her team members enjoying cake, their bright smiles clearly showing their joy in being acknowledged, appreciated, and celebrated. Jessica now knows the power of celebration and how much joy it unleashes in her and her team.

Celebration is not about you and what you like.

Laughter is a big part of celebration.

JOY PRACTICE:

1. Create a list of special days for your team, such as their birthdays, anniversaries, and achievements. Update it regularly and refer to it when you are planning your week.
2. Set the intention each day to celebrate someone or something. Decide what and how, and then make sure to do it.
3. Let people know how grateful you are for something they have done, or just for who they are. Make it very specific, and of course, true.
4. Laugh! It's said that children laugh over 300 times per day, whilst adults laugh an average of 15 times. Channel your inner child and laugh, not AT someone but WITH them.

Make celebration a conscious daily practice and watch the joy of your team flourish.

JOY JOURNALLING PROMPTS FOR CELEBRATION:

- What can I celebrate today?
- Who am I grateful for today?
- What's bringing me laughter and joy?

. . . AND REMEMBER:

Joy needs space

Joy is a serious value proposition

Joy is a choice

Joy regardless: for times when there's no space for **joy**, when **joy** doesn't seem to be of value and when it's difficult to choose it.

J

JOY REGARDLESS

Sharon, my dear friend, fellow Executive Coach, and Harvard Business School alumna, who lives in the United States, reached out to me a few months after George Floyd's death:

"Marguerite. Help me here. How can I be joyful in this whole George Floyd situation? Every time I see the video, I just feel despondent, angry, and hopeless."

I sighed. Because I, too, have felt that way. Most of us have felt deep despair that things are getting worse, not better, and are frankly traumatised by the barrage of injustice, pain, and suffering played out every day.

Sharon's question caused me to dig deep and to ask myself: Are we better served by despair or joy?

Archbishop Desmond Tutu, who to me is the personification of joy, despite living through the most heinous of experiences, once said:

"No dark fate determines our joy. We do."

At every moment, we are faced with choices – joy or what? What's the alternative to joy?

If we pay attention to the news, we will be convinced that the world is a never-ending deluge of despair, distress, tribulation, tragedy, mayhem, inequities, and injustice. Joy very rarely makes breaking news. Yet, by definition, the news is about the unusual, which suggests that there's way more good in humanity than what's reported. Every day we see this goodness – even in the George Floyd case – like Darnella Frazier, who stood steady for the 9 minutes and 29 seconds of his murder to record it for posterity. And then she testified at the trial of his killers, reliving over and over the experience of seeing a life snuffed out. What amazing courage! What grace in the face of evil and horror in someone so young.

Perhaps she, and people like her all over the world throughout history who have done good deeds, if asked, would not describe their actions as coming from joy. Yet their actions demonstrated the essence of joy – courage, compassion, kindness, caring, and hope. In the moment, this is what they chose.

But even as we recognise and celebrate this goodness, we cannot and should not deny our emotions of anger, despair, distress, and fear. These are valid and normal. We must have

"No dark fate determines our joy. **We do.**"

them, else we aren't human. But if we look only at the negative, we will have dismissed the good. It is because we acknowledge these emotions that we can move through them to compassion and then to action. The triumph is to be empowered by choosing hope, compassion, life, and yes, joy, and then to act from this place.

Finding joy means choosing joy, regardless . . . This takes courage, because it doesn't feel like the natural thing to do. It's uncomfortable. You might even feel guilty, as I have felt, asking myself what right do I have to feel joy when others are suffering? When a team member dies or is diagnosed with a life-threatening illness. When your business is on the verge of bankruptcy and ruin. Or when ethical misdeeds run rampant throughout your organisation, and are accepted as the norm, creating a highly toxic culture of mistrust, stress, and burnout.

Yet, in my heart, I know that joy is the only way because it's the way of hope. The same hope that kept my ancestors alive across the Middle Passage, through slavery and discrimination, so that I can be here today.

How can we make sure that we act from a place of joy, no matter what?

Hold a vision of a better world, a better nation, a better organisation, a better you, with conviction – believe it, speak it, even if you are laughed at in scorn. Doesn't matter. It's your vision. You have a right to it.

In times of despair, which will come, always remember that the darkest hour comes before the dawn.

Never forget that there's more good than evil in this world. Find and honour the goodness of humanity, and in particular, of the people with whom you interact.

And never let anyone steal your joy – because it is your own joy that will light the way for you to take decisive action that changes the world, and that inspires others to do the same. This is the essence of great leadership.

. . . it is your own joy that will **light the way for you** . . .

AND ALWAYS REMEMBER:

Joy needs space –
to shine and bring hope

Joy is a serious value proposition – it benefits your organisation, your community, your nation, and the world

Joy is a choice – at work, in your leadership, and in all aspects of your life

“**Joy** is
contagious”

J

CASCADING JOY

How to cascade joy throughout your organisation

As you develop your own practice of leading joyfully, are you becoming aware of the impact it is having on your team?

"Joy is a serious value proposition"

Are you ready for your organisation to start experiencing some of the results I mentioned in the Introduction, of having happy, engaged team members?

Are you ready to cascade joy throughout your organisation?

Are you ready to go even further and instill a culture of joy at work?

"**Joy** is a serious value proposition"

Imagine yourself as a pebble of joy tossed into a pond, rippling in concentric circles to your immediate team, their teams, customers, suppliers, and the wider community. This is truly what it means to lead with joy.

"Joy is a choice"

The place to begin is with your Leadership Team. Embrace the 8 Essential Practices together, working through one practice at a time. One approach my clients have found very helpful is a 20 to 30-minute session once per week, with a different member of the team leading a discussion on the practice for that week.

"**Joy** is a choice"

Here are some questions on each Practice that can guide the discussion:

PRACTICE #1: REFLECTION:

- What would joy at OUR workplace look like?
- What would relationships with each other be like? With our customers, suppliers, and the wider community?
- How would team members be behaving?
- What's helping or hindering joy at our workplace?
- How would we lead differently?
- What's one small, but significant action we can take as a team to cascade joy at work?

PRACTICE #2: GROUND YOUR DAY IN JOY:

- How do we start our collective day at work?
- How do we greet each other?
- How do we start meetings?
- What are our own organisational rituals i.e. the activities we collectively participate in each day?
- Do our practices help or hinder joy?
- What's one small, but significant action we can take as a team to collectively ground our day in joy?

PRACTICE #3: SILENCE:

- Are we allowing space in our conversations to really listen to our team members?
- How are we using our phones? Are they helping or hindering conversations?
- How are we using email? How are our email policies and practices helping or hindering joy?
- How well is our technology serving us, our team members, our customers, and suppliers?
- Are we being intentional about our use of technology?
- What's one small, but significant action we can take as a team to create space through silence?

PRACTICE #4: MAKE PEACE WITH TIME:

- How are we utilising our time as a team – are we focussing on our priorities, or on the minutiae?
- Is every meeting necessary, or are there other ways to accomplish what we intend? Is each one the best use of the time allotted?
- How productive are our meetings? Are they achieving the objectives? Do they start and end on time? Are the right people "in the room"?

- What's one small, but significant action we can take as a team to improve how we are spending our time and others' time?

PRACTICE #5: FORGIVENESS:

This may be the most difficult practice to discuss as it is very deeply personal and may bring to the surface long-concealed hurts. But it may be the most transformational, in terms of deepening the discussion about joy. Approach the topic with care and sensitivity:

- What is a previous experience at work that has hurt each of us, which we have not yet been able to release? Why was it so hurtful? Who hurt us? *Note that this does not have to have occurred at your organisation.*
- Are there people who have hurt or betrayed us as a team or organisation?
- Are there people that we may have hurt? Do we know if they are still hurting? Are we still carrying the guilt of our actions?
- What's one small, but significant action we can take as a team to forgive and release?

PRACTICE #6: ACCEPTANCE:

- Who in our team are we constantly judging and berating? Why? What might happen if we simply accepted them as they are? How might we behave differently with them? How might this change our relationship?
- How is our language signalling non-acceptance and judgement?
- What's one small, but significant action we can take as a team to accept our team members as they are, BUT without condoning any negative actions?

PRACTICE #7: ASK FOR HELP:

- What tasks are we carrying out that our team members could and should be doing, i.e. how well are we delegating?
- How can we ask them to help without overburdening them?
- What tasks are unnecessary for them (or anyone else) to do? i.e. what's redundant?
- What's stopping us from asking others to help?
- How vulnerable is this making us feel?
- What's one small, but significant action we can take as a team to ask for help?

PRACTICE #8: CELEBRATION:

- Are we celebrating the small accomplishments of each other and our team members?
- Are we genuinely expressing our gratitude?
- To what extent is laughter a part of our culture?
- What's one small, but significant action we can take as a team to celebrate more?

These questions are prompts to start a discussion and action. Approach them with patience and care. Revisit them regularly to deepen the conversations. Become aware of the impact these discussions and your actions are having on your team.

HOW MARGUERITE CAN HELP

Creating a workplace in which lasting joy flourishes takes time. Perhaps you have started to create space for joy around you and your team, and you know there's more to be done. Please also know, this is a big initiative, and you don't have to do it alone.

Remember Practice #7 – **Ask for Help**

Here are some of the ways I can support you:

- Speaking – my keynotes are an exciting, energising and impactful way to get the conversation on Leading with Joy started in your organisation, and in your industry associations.
- J.O.Y. (Journey Of You) Executive Leadership Coaching – highly personalised 6-month coaching programme.
- Nourish to Flourish – a highly interactive process for you and your team to get clear on what you want YOUR joyful workplace to be.
- Mindfulness Meditation Essentials – introduction of your team to Mindfulness Meditation, and techniques that encourage a short daily practice of silence and calm.

I'd love to hear from you to talk about how you might be able to cascade joy throughout your organisation so that you and your team will experience the results of a Culture of Joy.

And always remind yourself and each other:

Joy needs space

Joy is a serious value proposition

Joy is a choice

LEARN MORE ABOUT JOYFUL LEADERSHIP

Here are some of the books that have most influenced my thinking and practice of joy in general and at work:

The Book of Joy: Lasting Happiness in a Changing World – His Holiness the Dalai Lama and Archbishop Desmond Tutu with Douglas Abrams.

I was inspired and in awe of the conversations rooted in the deep friendship of the Dalai Lama and Archbishop Tutu, their love for each other, and the joy that bubbles over in their interactions. This book helped me begin to understand the nature of joy, what gets in the way of the human expression of joy, and how we can unleash more joy in our lives. The chapter on Forgiveness was particularly life-changing for me.

Maverick: The Success Story Behind the World's Most Unusual Workplace – Ricardo Semler

Ricardo Semler had a profound impact on how I view organisations. In "Maverick", he presents a different and revolutionary alternative to how we view people, trust and lead them, and organise to best support them. Recounting the experience of leading his family business in Brazil, I was particularly struck by Ricardo's non-North American worldview and experience. He challenged me to question everything I had learned at business school.

Chief Joy Officer: How Great Leaders Elevate Human Energy and Eliminate Fear – Richard Sheridan

The idea of Joy as the responsibility of the CEO helped me to see how important leadership at the highest level is. Richard Sheridan makes it clear that if you want joy at work, you have to be it and lead it, out loud and unapologetically.

Work as a Spiritual Practice: A Practical Buddhist Approach to Inner Growth and Satisfaction on the Job – Lewis Richmond

Could work really be an expression of our spirituality? This book challenged my thinking about the practice of separating spirituality and work. And if work is a spiritual practice, then so must leadership be.

The Prophet – Kahlil Gibran

Gibran's beautiful treatise on Work elevated my view of work to the highest level of human expression. My heart soars whenever I read this book. "Work is love made visible. And if you cannot work with love but only with distaste, it is better that you should leave your work and sit at the gate of the temple and take alms of those who work with joy."

Looptail: Why Community, Culture and Karma Matter in Business – Bruce Poon Tip

This book is particularly meaningful to me as I have actually experienced the culture about which Bruce Poon Tip writes, in my adventures with his company, G Adventures, in Tanzania (Mt. Kilimanjaro), Peru (The Inca Trail and Machu Picchu), Nepal (Annapurna Circuit Trek), Egypt, and India. Every CEO (Chief Experience Officer) lives the G Adventures values and culture, whilst being true to their own unique national identity. Total joy was my experience with each trek.

First Things First: To Live, to Love, to Learn, to Leave a Legacy – Stephen R. Covey

"Between stimulus and response, there is a space. In that space is our power to choose our response. In our response lies our growth and our freedom." This quote stimulated my thinking about the relationship between joy and space. Covey's simple, practical Priority Management Model is a mainstay in my coaching and leadership development practice.

> "Work is love made visible. And if you cannot work with love but only with distaste, it is better that you should leave your work and **sit at the gate of the temple and take alms of those who work with joy**."
>
> —KAHLIL GIBRAN

J

IN JOY AND GRATITUDE

(Acknowledgements)

Every experience in my life, every person with whom I have interacted, every book I have read, video I have viewed, podcast I have listened to, or speech I have heard, have all brought me to this time and place in my life. For all of these, I am truly grateful.

However, for this book I would like to say a big “love and tanks” to:

- My clients who trusted me when I started to express this crazy idea of joy as an integral part of work and leadership. Thanks for your full participation in our coaching, your all-out involvement in workshops that were fun AND serious, and your smiles, laughter, and words of kindness that affirm that I am on the right track. May you continue to know the joy of leadership.
- My team at Free and Laughing Inc. – Carole, Ulla, Silke, Teresa, Judi, Nick, Sarah, and others who come and go as projects require. Our interactions are a manifestation of my commitment to "ease, grace and joy". You truly make the work we do together joyful.
- Co-conspirators in the birthing of this book – my Editor Cecile Clayton; Book Designer Robert Harris; Graphic Artist Chris Cushman; photographer Jik-Reuben Pringle; Makeup Artist Cecile Burrowes-Samuels; Beta Readers Carole Orane-Andrade, Gena Cox, John Scott, Judi Hughes, Sarah Owen, Nigel Romano; Book Launch and Promotion Consultant Robbie Samuels. With you, this process was . . . joy!
- My beloved family who continues to support every crazy adventure I embark on, including writing this book. Brother, Douglas, is my role model on how to build and lead a global organisation – Grace Kennedy Limited – rooted in Jamaica, which expresses the excellence and joy of being authentically Jamaican. Sister, Carole, is my venting partner, my sidekick, and an extremely wise and loving voice that whispers "hold on a moment" throughout my life and for this book.

- My parents continue to inspire – mom, Daisy, lived love each day, and was unafraid to explore and learn deeply. Dad, Douglas, gave me confidence and strength through a very challenging relationship, but deep down, I know he was proud of me.
- My partner, Douglass, for whom I seem unable to do any wrong. Well, mostly. His love and quiet support in the wee hours gifted me the space for writing the book.
- My children, Marc, Victoria and Shane, with whom I have had my greatest leadership journey – our family. Thanks for being willing (and sometimes unwilling) recipients of my efforts, for challenging me, calling me out when I wasn't being true to my espoused values, and for allowing me to hone the practices that I share in this book. Together, our family is still a work-in-progress, but it does get more joyful by the day.
- And finally, but by no means least, my sweet doggie Sushi. Every day she expresses joy. One look at her reminds me what joy is about – love, acceptance, patience, walks, and lots of treats! Love is unconditional, and so is joy.
- To whoever reads this book, thank you. May you create space in your life for joy, may you realise the immense value that it brings, and may you always know, no matter the circumstance, that you can always choose joy.

May you create **space in your life for joy**, may you realise the immense value that it brings, and may you know, no matter the circumstance, that **you can always choose joy**.

Made in the USA
Coppell, TX
16 June 2026

81589954R00090